9.26-95

HOT & SPICY
SAUCES & SALSAS

SALLY GRIFFITHS

PHOTOGRAPHS BY
SIMON WHEELER

NEW YORK

CONTENTS

THE PANTRY

The recipes in this collection can be made with herbs, spices, and other ingredients currently available in most supermarkets or, in a few cases, specialty food shops. More than half can be executed without venturing beyond the front door if the following items are kept in store:

Legumes and Grains

Canned or dried black beans, red kidney beans, blackeyed peas, navy or cannellini beans, lentils, rice, couscous

Chilies

Dried hot chilies, fresh hot red and green chilies, chili powder, dried chili (hot pepper) flakes, cayenne, paprika

Fresh Herbs

Cilantro, mint, basil, parsley, chives

Fruit and Vegetables

Tomatoes, red bell peppers, green bell peppers, yellow bell peppers, cucumber, celery, garlic, shallots, onions, green onions, lemons, limes, oranges

General Ingredients

Brown sugar, white sugar, molasses, honey, dried apricots, coconut milk, cornstarch, dried marjoram, canned unsweetened pineapple, canned tomatoes, gherkins, capers, white wine, sherry, red currant jelly, peanut butter

In the Refrigerator

Plain yogurt, crème fraîche, eggs, butter

In the Freezer

Containers of homemade beef, chicken, and vegetable stock

Nuts

Once the package has been opened, store in an airtight container.
Cashew nuts, pine nuts, walnuts, peanuts, pistachio nuts

Oils

Store in a cool, dark place.
Sunflower, olive, sesame, peanut, walnut

Pastes

Unopened paste will last indefinitely. Once open, use as quickly as possible. Store in the refrigerator.
Thai red curry paste, Thai green curry paste, tomato paste, Indian curry paste

Sauces

Japanese soy sauce, Tabasco, West Indian hot pepper sauce

Spices

Allspice, caraway seeds, cardamom pods, cinnamon, cloves, ground coriander, coriander seeds, ground cumin, cumin seeds, curry powder, fennel seeds, garam masala, fresh gingerroot, lemon grass, dry mustard, mace, black mustard seeds, black peppercorns, green peppercorns in brine, salt, nutmeg, poppy seeds, saffron, sesame seeds, turmeric

Vinegars

Balsamic vinegar, rice wine vinegar, malt or cider vinegar, white wine vinegar

CHILIES

Originally from Central and South America, chilies, or hot peppers, have been used as a food ingredient for at least 8,000 years, and were introduced to the rest of the world by the Portuguese and Spaniards in the 16th and 17th centuries. There are hundreds of different varieties grown all over the world, each with its own individual flavor and heat level. Chilies are without question the most important ingredient in almost all hot and spicy recipes.

What is the difference between red and green chilies? Most chilies are green in their unripened state. As they ripen they become red, yellow, orange, or brown. In general, the redder the chili, the sweeter the taste.

How can you tell a hot chili from a mild one? It really is a question of experimentation, although there are some guidelines. See pages 10-11 on fresh and dried chilies.

Which is the best way to keep fresh chilies? Wash, dry, wrap them in paper towels (not plastic bags, which create moisture and hasten the spoiling process), and store in the refrigerator. Kept in the open, chilies will quickly shrivel and lose their flavor.

What should you look for when buying fresh chilies? Choose brightly colored, firm, unblemished chilies with smooth, unbroken skins. A sharp, clean smell is indicative of good fresh chilies.

Are fresh chilies used with or without their seeds? It largely depends on how hot you want the sauce to be. However, it is the vein to which the seeds are attached that holds much of the heat, so when removing seeds, take care to cut out the vein as well.

Do chilies irritate the skin? Yes. Chilies contain capsaicin, an oil that can cause skin irritation. Wash the afflicted area immediately with soapy water, and always wear rubber gloves when handling large quantities of chilies.

Can you freeze fresh chilies? Wash and dry fresh, good-quality chilies, then split them in half, remove seeds, chop, and lay flat on a tray. Put the tray in the freezer and, when the pieces are frozen, store them in plastic bags. Thaw frozen chilies before using.

Roasted chilies can be frozen whole—the skins will come off easily when they are thawed.

Can you reduce the heat level of chilies? Eating a hot chili can take your breath away! A glass of water will cool you down temporarily, but try beer or some kind of spirit for longer-lasting relief.

Cooking chilies (by roasting, frying, or grilling) will reduce the heat level, as will sugar, dairy products such as yogurt, milk, or ice cream, or bananas and coconut milk.

What is the advantage of dried chilies? They are always on hand when you need them. The process of drying chilies concentrates the sugars and flavors, making them more a spice.

How long can you keep dried chilies? Store in a plastic bag in the freezer for 1-2 years, or keep in an airtight container in a cool, dry, dark place for 8 months to a year maximum.

How do you know which chili to buy when a recipe simply indicates "chilies?" In this book every recipe has a heat level indicated in parentheses beside the heading, for example: Green Chutney Sauce (mild-medium).

You can then refer to the sections on fresh and dried chilies for the heat of each chili—i.e. Anaheim green (mild-medium). The trick is to become acquainted with your own preferred heat level and to experiment accordingly.

How do you know when to use dried or fresh chilies? Some recipes require fresh chilies, others call for dried. Very often it is simply a matter of choice or availability.

As a general guide, fresh chilies give a mild flavor and a wonderful crunch in salsas and other fresh sauces, whereas dried chilies, which have a more distinctive flavor, are used mostly in sauces, stews, and purées.

How do you adjust the heat of your sauce? If a sauce is too hot, tone it down with rice, potatoes, dairy products, coconut milk, or a touch of sugar.

FRESH CHILIES

Most of the fresh chilies listed below can be found in large supermarkets, specialty food shops, and Latin and Asian markets, according to seasonal availability.

Anaheim *green – mild*

Also known as the long green chili, New Mexico, Rio Grande, or California chili. About 6-8 inches in length and slender, with a distinct vegetable flavor. Traditionally used to make *chiles rellenos;* also good in stews and sauces. Also available canned.

Chilaca *dark green/dark brown – medium*

Long chili (6-8 inches), often curved. Rich flavor. Usually roasted and peeled before use. When dried this chili is called a pasilla.

Fresno *lightish-green – medium-hot*

Medium-small chili, often mistaken for the jalapeño. Excellent in salsas, pickled, or roasted and blended into sauces.

Fresno *cherry red – medium-hot*

The mature Fresno, which looks very like the mature Santa Fe Grande. Sweeter than the green Fresno.

Habañero *light green or yellow – very hot*

The hottest chili in the world. Lantern-shaped, it measures about 2 inches in length. Use in salsas, seafood marinades, and chutneys.

Habañero *orange or red – very hot*

Riper and sweeter than the green habañero.

Jalapeño *green – medium*

Probably the most commonly used chili. Thick-fleshed, about 2 inches long, with a green vegetable flavor. Use it to spike up salsas, dips, stews, and sauces. Also available canned and pickled.

Jalapeño *red – medium*

The mature jalapeño, which has a sweeter flavor than the green jalapeño. When smoked, the jalapeño is called a chipotle chili and can be found in cans or jars.

New Mexico Red *red – mild*

Also known as the long red chili, this is the red strain of the green Anaheim chili. Very versatile and sweeter than its green counterpart. Use in sauces, soups, and stews.

Poblano *dark green with purple-black tinge – mild*

Measures 4–6 inches in length, with a thick flesh. Usually roasted and peeled before use in recipes. When dried this is called an ancho chili.

Santa Fe Grande *yellow/pale green – hot*

Short, cone-shaped chili with a fresh, light flavor and sharp refined heat. Also called caribe and caloro, sometimes güero.

Santa Fe Grande *pink/red – hot-very hot*

Riper and sweeter than the yellow Santa Fe Grande.

Scotch Bonnet *yellow-green, orange and red – very hot*

Also called West Indian chili. Similar in appearance to the habañero, it has a distinctive smoky flavor. Used in many Caribbean dishes.

Serrano *bright green – hot*

Slender, about 2 inches long. A clean, biting heat. Perfect for salads or in raw or cooked sauces. Also sold pickled

Serrano *red – hot*

Riper and sweeter than the green serrano.

Thai *bright green, or red when ripe – hot*

Measures about 1 1/2 inches in length and used mostly in Southeast Asian cooking. Similar small chilies are the cayenne and arbol, both of which are slightly less hot than the Thai.

Wax *yellow – mild-medium*

Also called Hungarian wax pepper and banana pepper. Long, slim chili with a pungent flavor. Perfect for salads or sauces.

Wax *red-orange – mild-medium*

Riper and sweeter than the yellow wax pepper.

DRIED CHILIES

As they dry the flavor of chilies intensifies, resulting in a distinctive smell and taste. Select clean, unbroken chilies with bright colors and a good aroma. Most dried chilies need to be reconstituted before use by soaking in hot water for 20 minutes. Then chop, shred, or purée with a little of the soaking liquid until a moderately thick consistency is formed, or prepare according to recipe directions.

Anaheim *dark green – mild-medium*

Peeled, roasted and dried version of the fresh green Anaheim or California chili. Has a sweet, smoky taste tinged with flavors of celery and dried apple. Use in powdered form to season soups and stews. Remove stem and soak, then shred or chop and add to the cooking pot.

Ancho *reddish-black – mild*

This ripened and dried form of the poblano is the most commonly used chili in Mexico. Sweet and fruity. Excellent for stuffing. Also available in powdered form. Remove stem and seeds and soak; split before stuffing. There is no need to peel.

Bird's Eye *bright orange – very hot*

Small, East African chili with a sharp black pepper taste. Good whole —rather like a bay leaf—in soups, stews, and piri piri sauces and for flavoring vinegars and oil. Can be crushed in a pestle and mortar.

Cascabel/cascabelle *dark reddish-brown – medium*

Small round chili also known as "little rattle" because of the sound it makes when shaken. It has a mild, nutty, woody flavor and is good in stews, soups, sauces, and salsas. Remove stem and seeds and soak, then scoop out the flesh with a teaspoon and mash with other ingredients.

Chipotle *coffee-brown – medium-hot*

A ripened and smoked jalapeño, this is sold both dried and pickled. It has a sweet nutty flavor and is widely used in Mexican cooking. Remove stem, soak, remove seeds, and purée with a little of the soaking liquid.

Choricero *dark reddish-brown – mild*

Large, very mild Spanish chili, suitable for stuffing. Use to flavor soups, seafood dishes, stews, sauces, and rice and bean dishes. Remove stem and seeds and soak, then purée with a little of the soaking liquid.

Guajillo *dark reddish-brown – mild-medium*

About 4 inches long, narrow, and slightly curved, this chili has a green tea flavor. Use in salsas and sauces. Remove stem and seeds and soak, then purée with a little of the soaking liquid and press through a strainer.

Guindilla *deep red – medium*

Spanish chili with a sweet flavor. Adds zip to sauces, stews, and soups. Can be toasted (see page 14). Remove stem and seeds and soak, then purée with a little of the soaking liquid and press through a strainer.

Habañero *yellow-orange – very hot*

Dried form of the fresh habañero and very, very hot. Great in condiments, fish stews, curries, and salsas. Remove stem and seeds and soak, then purée with a little of the soaking liquid. To flavor a dish during cooking, dried habañeros can be added whole, then removed once the desired heat is acquired.

New Mexico Red *dark red – mild*

This dried form of the fresh New Mexico red chili has a clean heat and an earthy, fruity flavor. Wonderful in red sauces. Dried New Mexico red chilies are ground for chili powder and paprika. Remove stem and soak, then purée with a little of the soaking water and press through a strainer.

Pasado *dull orange-red – medium*

This is a New Mexico red chili that has been roasted, then skinned and dried. It has a toasted flavor tinged with apple, celery, and citrus. Good in soups and stews. Remove stem and soak.

Pasilla *very dark brown – medium*

Long, thin, and wrinkled, this dried form of the chilaca chili tastes of berries and licorice. Good with seafood and in sauces. Often ground before use. Remove stem, shake out seeds, and soak, then purée in a little of the soaking water or chop.

Tepin *red – very hot*

Small spherical shape, with a searing heat. This chili has a dry, dusty flavor with a hint of corn and nuts. Remove stem, then crush onto food or use in cooking like a bay leaf.

Powdered and Crushed Dried Chilies:

Chimayo *medium* very finely ground Mexican chili. Sweet warm flavor. **Pequin** or **Piquin** *hot* also called chiles quebrados. Crushed. **Pimenton de la Vera** *hot* finely ground Spanish oak-smoked chilies.

SPICES

Store spices in airtight containers in a cool, dark place. Buy in small quantities for optimum freshness.

Allspice

Grown mostly in Jamaica, its name aptly describes the flavor: a combination of cinnamon, cloves, pepper, and nutmeg. Taken to Europe by the Spaniards in the 16th century, allspice is now used in cooking all over the world. The unripe green berries (the size of small peas) are dried in the sun and are only ready for use when they turn brown. To grind allspice, use a pestle and mortar, fine grater or spice mill. Also available ground.

Black Peppercorns

Pepper is the king of spices and was once literally worth its weight in gold. It accounts for one-quarter of the world's spice trade and India is the foremost producer. Black peppercorns are unripe green peppercorns that are left to ferment for a few days before being sun-dried. Freshly ground black pepper is used in many recipes. It has a strong, pungent flavor.

Caraway

Has been used as a spice since the Stone Age. The small, dried seeds are brown and have a distinctive aromatic and spicy flavor. Delicious with vegetables and rich meats, and in cakes and breads. Caraway is mainly used in seed form but is also available ground.

Cardamom

The third most expensive spice in the world and grown extensively in India, Mexico, and Guatemala, cardamom is an important ingredient in Indian cooking, especially in pilafs and curries. In the Middle East and North Africa, it is used to flavor sweetmeats, pastries, and strong black coffee. Green cardamom pods are the most common and have a strong, lemony taste that enhances the flavor of both savory and sweet dishes. Pods retain their flavor better than ground cardamom.

Cayenne

A very pungent spice ground from small ripe chilies of the *Capsicum frutescens* variety. It has been used in Western cooking since the 18th century.

Cinnamon

Native of Sri Lanka and now grown in many other wet, tropical countries. One of the oldest spices, it is the bark of a small evergreen tree which is peeled, rolled, and then dried. It has a pleasant woody aroma and a warm, fragrant taste. In Europe, cinnamon is used mainly in cakes, cookies, and sweet dishes, while in the Middle East, it is used to flavor savory dishes such as stews and curries.

Cloves

The name comes from the Latin *clavus*, meaning nail. Indeed these dried, unopened flower buds, native to the Spice Islands, do resemble nails. Grown in a tropical, maritime climate, cloves are aromatic but bitter on their own. Once cooked they give rich, instantly recognizable flavor in cakes, cookies, and mulled wine. Cloves also are used to flavor meat dishes, chutneys, and marinades.

Coriander

Native to southern Europe and the Middle East, coriander is a member of the carrot family and is used in cooking all over the world. In India, both leaves and seeds are used extensively in curries. Moroccan seeds, more commonly available here, have a milder taste than the Indian variety and a spicy aroma.

Cumin

Grown in many warm countries and used extensively in Indian, North African, Middle Eastern, and Mexican cooking. It has a distinctive warm, savory flavor, which is excellent in curries, couscous, and poultry and meat stews. Seeds can be used whole, or ground in a mortar just before use.

Curry Powder

May be a strong or mild mixture of various ground spices. There is no one specific blend—each powder is mixed according to taste and use and includes spices native to India, such as cinnamon, cloves, pepper, coriander, cumin, chilies, and turmeric.

Fennel Seeds

Have been used for thousands of years. They have a warm fragrant flavor with a strong taste of anise. For years fennel has been used to enhance the flavor of fresh fish, in pickles, and as an important ingredient in Indian vegetarian dishes.

Galangal

Native to Indonesia and southern China, and closely related to the ginger family. It is a knobbly root that comes in two types: lesser and greater. Lesser galangal tastes like cardamom and ginger; greater galangal is similar to a mixture of ginger and pepper. Lesser galangal is used as a vegetable in Southeast Asia, while greater galangal, available fresh, dried, or ground, is used in curries, stews, and coconut-based sauces. Fresh gingerroot can be substituted. Store fresh galangal in a plastic bag in the refrigerator, dry galangal in an airtight container in a cool, dark place.

Garam Masala

A traditional spice mixture from Northern India (masala means "mixture of spices"). There are literally hundreds of different masalas, each made from a combination of herbs and spices (cumin, coriander seeds, cinnamon, mace, cardamom, black peppercorns, and bay leaf, for example). Other masalas based on pepper and cloves are much hotter. Use garam masala sparingly to flavor pilafs, birianis, and meat dishes, or sprinkle on food before serving.

Ginger

A knobbly root used extensively in most Asian cuisines, where it is considered almost as important as salt. It is a versatile spice with a clean, fresh taste that enhances the flavors of both sweet and savory dishes. Choose firm roots and keep wrapped in a paper towel in a plastic bag, in the refrigerator.

Mustard

A hot spice that derives from the cabbage family. White mustard seeds are used as a pickling spice, and brown mustard seeds are an important flavoring in Indian cooking.

Nutmeg and Mace

Myristica fragrans is a unique plant because it produces two different spices under one shell. Mace is the lacy covering that surrounds the seed, the nutmeg. Nutmeg and mace have similar aromas and flavors, although mace is slightly more refined. Nutmeg is used in sauces and custards and with vegetables and stewed fruits, while mace is used to flavor soups, sauces, fish and poultry dishes, cakes, desserts, and custards. Freshly grated nutmeg has infinitely more flavor than ready ground.

Paprika

Made from particular ground dried sweet or hot peppers. Originally from Mexico, the plants found their way to Hungary where paprika soon became an essential part of the cuisine. Paprika has a lightly pungent, sweet or hot flavor (according to the peppers used), and is added to a wide variety of dishes including stews, soups, and cream-based sauces. Paprika loses its flavor and aroma quickly, so buy it in small quantities.

Poppy Seeds

Native to the Middle East, these are the ripe seeds of the opium poppy. They have a nutty aroma and texture, which is vastly improved by toasting. Delicious in breads, cookies and cakes, curries, and sauces. Grind the seeds in a mortar or spice mill.

Saffron

The hand-picked stamens of more than 250,000 crocus flowers are needed to yield one pound of saffron—which explains why it is the world's most expensive spice. Used as a spice since the 10th century, it is produced mostly in Spain. Saffron threads are highly aromatic and preferable to ground saffron, which quickly loses its flavor; the deeper the color, the better the quality. Saffron has a strong yellow color and is indispensable in many sauces, stews, and fish dishes such as bouillabaisse and paella. Buy in small quantities because saffron quickly loses its flavor.

Salt

Once valued so highly that it was used as an offering to the gods, today it is a relatively cheap commodity. Salt is used to season and preserve food and also acts as a precious nutrient for the body. There are two types of salt: rock salt and sea salt. Sea salt is definitely more powerful than rock salt, so use it carefully. To absorb dampness, mix a few grains of rice with salt.

Sesame Seeds

These come in three varieties: white, brown, or black. They contain 50 per cent oil, and have a lovely nutty flavor that is enhanced by toasting (see below). Sesame seeds add a crunchy texture to sweet and savory dishes, such as breads, cakes, and cookies, or rice, vegetables, and salad dressings.

Star Anise

A small, star-shaped fruit with an aroma and flavor similar to anise. It is used extensively in Chinese and Vietnamese cooking, and is an essential ingredient in Chinese five-spice powder. Star anise will keep indefinitely in an airtight container, away from the light. Grind it in a mortar or spice mill.

Tamarind

Has been cultivated in India for centuries and was probably taken to Europe in the 15th century by the Crusaders. It has a slightly sour, fruity flavor, with a pleasant sweet aroma, and is used to flavor curries, vegetable stews, and chutneys, or in any recipe needing a slight sourness. Tamarind concentrate is difficult to find but is more economical than fresh. Store in a plastic bag in the refrigerator.

Turmeric

A member of the ginger family which has been cultivated for thousands of years in tropical areas. Dried or ground, turmeric is an important ingredient in curry powders. It is also used to flavor pickles and many Indian vegetarian dishes. Turmeric can be used as a substitute for saffron, but while it will give a similar deep yellow color to a dish, it does not have the same, pungent flavor.

HOW TO:

Toast nuts, seeds, and coconut Toss them around in a hot, dry skillet until they are lightly browned. Be careful not to burn them.

Peel tomatoes Put the tomatoes in a large bowl of boiling water and let stand for 1-2 minutes. Remove the tomatoes from the water and peel—and the skin will come off easily.

Peel bell peppers and chilies Put them under the broiler, skin side up, until the skins blister and turn black. Then remove and put them immediately into a plastic bag and seal. Cool the peppers, then pull off the skin.

Reconstitute dried chilies Soak them in hot water for 20 minutes, then chop, shred, or purée according to the type of chili and recipe instructions.

SAUCES

All recipes are for four portions.

SPICY CHICKPEA SAUCE MEDIUM-HOT

This sauce is delicious served with naan bread or as a side dish with curry. It is good with merguez sausages, too.

3 cloves garlic, peeled
2-inch piece fresh gingerroot, peeled and roughly chopped
1 fresh medium-hot red chili, or 1 dried chipotle chili, soaked (see page 11), or 1 dried guajillo chili, soaked, puréed, and sieved (see page 11)
1 teaspoon cumin seeds

1 teaspoon garam masala
2 tablespoons sunflower oil
1 red onion, chopped
1 can (16-ounce) chickpeas (garbanzo beans), with their juice, roughly chopped in the blender
1/4 cup chopped fresh cilantro
Salt and freshly ground black pepper

Place the garlic, gingerroot, chili, cumin seeds, and garam masala in a blender and roughly chop for a few seconds.

Heat the oil in a heavy pan over medium heat, stir in the chopped mixture, and gently warm through. Add the onion and cook for 2 minutes, then add the chickpeas and simmer for 10 minutes. Stir in the cilantro and season to taste with salt and pepper.

• If the mixture gets too thick, add a little more water.

LEMON AND CASHEW SAUCE

MILD AND AROMATIC

A delicate, slightly aromatic sauce. Serve stirred into wild or basmati rice.

2/3 cup cashew nuts roughly chopped in the blender
1 teaspoon mustard seeds
1/2 teaspoon turmeric
Juice of 3 lemons

Grated rind of 2 lemons
1 teaspoon chopped dried curry leaf
2 tablespoons sherry
1 teaspoon honey
Salt and freshly ground black pepper

Place the cashew nuts and mustard seeds in a hot pan and toast over medium heat for 4-6 minutes or until they brown slightly. Shake the pan frequently.

Add the rest of the ingredients and bring to a boil.

Season to taste with salt and pepper and serve.

NEW ORLEANS RED-BEAN SAUCE

MEDIUM-HOT

This is a traditional Cajun dish. Serve with bowls of fluffy white rice.

3 tablespoons extra virgin olive oil
6 cloves garlic, peeled and chopped
4 tomatoes, chopped
1 red bell pepper, chopped
15 okra, sliced into 1/4-inch rounds

2 bay leaves
1 tablespoon West Indian hot pepper sauce
1 can (16-ounce) red kidney beans with their juice
Salt and freshly ground black pepper

Heat the oil in a heavy pan over medium heat and gently sauté the garlic for 1-2 minutes. Add the tomatoes, bell pepper, okra, bay leaves, and hot pepper sauce and cook for 5 minutes.

Add the beans and simmer for a further 5 minutes.

Season with salt and pepper and serve.

GUJARATI VEGETABLE AND BEAN SAUCE MEDIUM-HOT

A robust, gutsy sauce based on an authentic Indian recipe. Serve with rice or barbecued chicken.

2-3 tablespoons sunflower oil
2 fresh medium-hot green chilies, minced, or 2 dried guindilla chilies, soaked, puréed, and sieved (see page 11)
1 teaspoon turmeric
1 teaspoon black mustard seeds
1 teaspoon cumin seeds
2-inch piece fresh gingerroot, peeled and chopped

1 can (16-ounce) yellow split peas with their juice
1 cup canned brown lentils with their juice
1 cup canned blackeyed peas
1/2 eggplant, finely chopped (not peeled)
1/2 red bell pepper, minced
Juice of 1 lime
Salt and freshly ground black pepper

Heat the oil in a heavy pan over medium heat, add the chilies, turmeric, mustard seeds, cumin seeds, and gingerroot, and gently warm through for 1-2 minutes, taking care not to burn the ingredients.

Add the split peas, lentils, blackeyed peas, and vegetables. Bring to a boil, and simmer for 8 minutes.

Stir in the lime juice and season to taste with salt and pepper.

• To make this sauce into a delicious soup, add 2 1/2 cups of good stock.

Right: Persian Sauce

PERSIAN SAUCE AROMATIC AND SPICY

Bursting with exotic Middle Eastern flavors and aromas, this pungent sauce is excellent on its own or mixed with rice.

4 cardamom pods
1/2 teaspoon ground cloves
1/2 teaspoon caraway seeds
5 saffron threads
3 tablespoons shelled pistachio nuts
1 heaped tablespoon slivered almonds,
toasted (see page 14)
6 fresh dates, pitted

3 tablespoons chopped dried apricots,
or chopped zaradaloo
(Middle Eastern dried apricots
with honey)
1 tablespoon Pernod
Seeds of 1 pomegranate
Juice of 2 oranges
2 tablespoons water

Put all the ingredients, except the Pernod, pomegranate seeds, orange juice, and water, in a food processor and blend for a few seconds.

Transfer the mixture to a bowl and stir in the water, Pernod, orange juice, and pomegranate seeds.

INDONESIAN COCONUT SAUCE

MILD AND AROMATIC

This is a wonderful Indonesian recipe. Mix with boiled white or Thai fragrant rice. Alternatively, try it with grilled fish or shrimp, or cook the fish in the sauce.

1-inch piece dried galangal, grated
2-inch piece fresh gingerroot,
peeled and chopped
Flesh (and juice) of 1 coconut, chopped, or
1/2 cup canned unsweetened coconut milk

12 fennel seeds
2/3 cup water
Juice of 1/2 lime
1 heaped tablespoon chopped fresh cilantro
Salt and freshly ground black pepper

Put the galangal, gingerroot, coconut, fennel seeds, and half the water in a food processor and blend to a liquid paste. Then, with the motor still running, add the rest of the water.

Transfer the mixture to a saucepan and, over medium heat, slowly bring to a boil. Remove from the heat and stir in the cilantro and lime juice.

Season to taste with salt and pepper.

SAG DHAL VERY HOT

Serve with flat Indian bread such as chapati or boiled new potatoes, or as an accompaniment to korma dishes. On its own, Sag Dhal makes a wonderful vegetable dish.

6 cloves garlic, peeled
2 fresh very hot green chilies, or 1 dried
habañero chili, soaked (see page 11), or
5 dried bird's eye chilies, crushed
2-inch piece fresh gingerroot, peeled
3 tablespoons olive oil
1 teaspoon cumin seeds

12 cardamom pods
1 1/2 teaspoons mild curry powder
1 can (16-ounce) green or brown lentils,
drained
2/3 cup water
1/2 pound fresh young spinach leaves
Fresh cilantro leaves
Salt and freshly ground black pepper

Put the garlic, chilies, and gingerroot in a blender and grind until a smooth paste is formed.

Heat the oil in a heavy pan and cook the paste with the cumin seeds, cardamom pods, and curry powder for 3-4 minutes.

Add the lentils, water, and spinach and bring to a boil. Simmer for 2-3 minutes.

Transfer the mixture to a food processor and blend until smooth. Sprinkle with cilantro and season to taste with salt and pepper.

• To cool the sauce down, add a little plain yogurt.

GREEN MEXICAN SAUCE HOT AND SOUR

This is a typical Mexican sauce. Serve with tortillas or beef hash, or stirred into rice.

1 stalk celery, roughly chopped
1 small onion, roughly chopped
2 green bell peppers, roughly chopped
6 cloves garlic, peeled and roughly chopped
3 fresh hot green chilies, seeded,
or 1 dried pasado chili, soaked
(see page 11) and roughly chopped
2 tablespoons oil

1/2 cup chopped fresh cilantro
1 teaspoon ground cumin
1 teaspoon mixed dried herbs such as
oregano and thyme
Juice of 1 lime
2/3 cup water
Salt and freshly ground black pepper

Put the celery, onion, bell peppers, garlic, and chilies in a food processor and blend until minced.

Heat the oil in a heavy-based pan and fry the minced vegetables until soft, 3-4 minutes.

Add the cilantro, cumin, mixed herbs, lime juice, and water, heat through, and stir together well.

Season to taste with salt and pepper.

Left: Spicy Chickpea Sauce

GREEN LENTIL DHAL HOT

Serve with Indian flat breads such as chapatis, with rice, or to accompany curry. Alternatively, Green Lentil Dhal makes an excellent dish on its own.

4 cloves garlic, peeled and chopped
1 1/4 cups chopped onions
2 fresh very hot chilies, chopped, or
2 dried bird's eye chilies, soaked
(see page 11) and chopped
3 tablespoons olive oil

2 tablespoons chopped fresh cilantro
1 tablespoon garam masala
6 cardamom pods
1 can (16-ounce) green lentils
with their juice
Salt and freshly ground black pepper

Put the garlic, onions, and chilies in a food processor and mince.

Heat the oil in a heavy pan over medium heat and fry the minced vegetables for 2-3 minutes. Add the remaining ingredients and simmer for 10 minutes.

Season to taste with salt and pepper.

• If the sauce is too thick, add a little water.

• To make a lovely, gutsy soup, add 2 1/2 cups of good chicken stock.

BELL-PEPPER SAUCE MILD

A delicious combination of tomatoes, chilies, bell peppers, and fresh herbs. Mix the sauce with green beans or white cannellini beans, or toss with hot pasta.

2 tablespoons olive oil
4 cloves garlic, peeled and chopped
1/2 onion, chopped
1 fresh mild red chili, chopped, or 1 dried
ancho chili (no need to soak), chopped
1 yellow bell pepper, cut into 1/4-inch dice

1 red bell pepper, cut into 1/4 inch dice
1 large ripe tomato, chopped
1/4 cup chopped fresh basil, or 1 cup
canned crushed tomatoes
3 tablespoons chopped fresh oregano
Salt and freshly ground black pepper

Heat the oil in a heavy pan and sauté the garlic, onion, and chili for 1-2 minutes. Add the bell peppers, tomato, and herbs and simmer until the bell peppers are soft, 8-10 minutes longer.

Transfer the mixture to a food processor and blend for 30 seconds. Season with salt and pepper and serve.

SPICED BULGAR WHEAT MILD

Much more than a sauce, this is a meal on its own. Or serve it over a platter of cooked black beans.

2/3 cup bulgar wheat
2 1/2 cups boiling water
1/4 cup olive oil
1 red bell pepper, chopped
Grated rind and juice of 1 lemon
2 cloves garlic, peeled and chopped
1 teaspoon ground cumin

1/2 teaspoon caraway seeds
1/2 teaspoon fennel seeds
Pinch of ground cloves
1 heaped tablespoon chopped fresh
flat-leaf parsley
Salt and freshly ground black pepper

Simmer the bulgar wheat in the boiling water for 10-15 minutes. Drain and set aside.

Heat the oil in a heavy pan and sauté the bell pepper with the lemon rind and juice, garlic, cumin, caraway seeds, fennel seeds, and cloves for 2-3 minutes. Then remove from the heat and stir in the bulgar wheat and parsley. Season with salt and pepper and serve.

• This makes an excellent cold dish, too.

HOT-PEPPER VINAIGRETTE HOT

This is a wonderfully light, tangy dressing. Serve with cold green beans, mushroom salad, artichoke hearts, or tossed with cold pasta.

1/4 cup extra virgin olive oil
1 tablespoon white wine vinegar
1 teaspoon Dijon mustard
2 tablespoons sun-dried tomato paste

2 tablespoons tomato paste
4 drops Tabasco sauce
Salt and freshly ground black pepper

Put all the ingredients in a bowl and mix together well.

PEPPER JELLY MILD-MEDIUM

A lovely, colorful jelly. Just the thing to accompany lamb, beef, ham, or packages of cheese wrapped and baked in filo pastry.

1 pound red currant or quince jelly	1 envelope unflavored gelatin, dissolved in
1 tablespoon mixed peppercorns, ground	3 tablespoons hot water (not boiling)

In a saucepan over medium heat, melt the jelly. Stir in the peppercorns and dissolved gelatin, then pour the liquid jelly into a container and refrigerate until set, about 2 hours. Spoon into a dish and serve.

EGGPLANT AND MINT SAUCE COOL

A refreshing, minty sauce and a tasty dish on its own, too. Serve with toasted pitta bread, over a tomato salad or boiled or steamed potatoes, or as an accompaniment to lamb or beef curry.

Preheat the oven to 400°F.

1 eggplant	1 teaspoon ground cinnamon
2 tablespoons chopped fresh mint	Salt and freshly ground black pepper
1 teaspoon sugar	

Place the eggplant in a small baking pan and cook in the oven for about 1 hour or until soft.

Remove the eggplant from the oven and cool for a few minutes, then scoop out the flesh into a small bowl. Discard the skin. Using a fork, mash the flesh into a purée.

Put all the ingredients (including the eggplant) in a bowl and mix together well. Season to taste with salt and pepper.

Serve hot or cold.

SPICED HERB DRESSING SPICY

Bursting with flavor, this gutsy sauce will spike up any salad, vegetable, or rice dish.

3 tablespoons chopped fresh basil	1 teaspoon cumin seeds
3 tablespoons fresh tarragon leaves	1/2 cup light olive oil
3 tablespoons chopped fresh parsley	Grated rind and juice of 1/2 lemon
3 tablespoons chopped fresh chives	1/4 teaspoon salt
1 teaspoon fennel seeds	Freshly ground black pepper

Put all the ingredients in a bowl and mix together well. Season to taste with pepper.

POPPY-SEED DRESSING MILD

This dressing has a piquant flavor and is delicious with a green leaf, raw carrot, or Chinese noodle salad.

1/4 cup sunflower oil	2 tablespoons poppy seeds
1/4 cup orange juice	1/4 teaspoon salt
1 teaspoon grated orange rind	1/4 teaspoon freshly ground black pepper

Put all the ingredients in a screw-top jar and shake well.

LOVAGE AND LIME SAUCE MILD

Simple to make, this sauce perfectly complements a fresh green or hot potato salad.

1 tablespoon chopped fresh mint	1/4 cup sunflower oil
1 tablespoon chopped fresh cilantro	1 tablespoon lime juice
1 tablespoon chopped fresh lovage or	1/2 teaspoon Dijon mustard
celery leaves	1/4 teaspoon salt
1 fresh green jalapeño chili, minced	1/4 teaspoon freshly ground black pepper

Put all the ingredients in a food processor and blend until fine.

HOT BASIL DRESSING MEDIUM

Try this fresh-flavored, nutty dressing over hot or cold Chinese noodles, grilled tomatoes, whole globe artichokes, broccoli, or cauliflower.

1/3 cup chopped fresh basil	2 tablespoons sunflower oil
2 heaped tablespoons walnut pieces	Juice of 1/2 lemon
1 fresh green jalapeño chili, or 1/2 dried	1/4 teaspoon salt
pasilla chili, soaked (see page 11)	1/4 teaspoon freshly ground black pepper
2 tablespoons walnut oil	

Put all the ingredients in a food processor and blend until fine.

COCONUT AND CHILI SAUCE

MEDIUM-HOT AND AROMATIC

A smooth, creamy sauce, delicious over hard-boiled eggs, mixed vegetables, root vegetables, or rice.

2 onions, quartered	5 cloves garlic, peeled
3-inch piece fresh gingerroot, peeled	2 teaspoons garam masala or curry powder
and cut into 1-inch slices	1/4 teaspoon salt
2 fresh green jalapeño chilies, chopped, or	1/4 teaspoon freshly ground pepper
2 dried chipotle chilies, soaked (see page 11)	2 tablespoons peanut oil
and chopped, or 2 guajillo chilies, soaked,	2 tablespoons sunflower oil
puréed, and sieved (see page 11)	1 can (14-ounce) unsweetened coconut milk

Put all the ingredients, except the oils and coconut milk, into the food processor and blend until smooth. Heat the oils in a heavy pan over medium heat and sauté the processed mixture for 2 minutes, stirring constantly. Add the coconut milk and simmer for 5 minutes.

Season to taste with salt and pepper.

GADO GADO SAUCE MEDIUM-HOT

This is a hot, crunchy sauce that complements deep-fried bean curd, bean sprouts, pak choy, and many other Asian vegetables to perfection. Alternatively, try it with a cold chicken salad.

2 tablespoons sesame oil
2 fresh medium-hot red chilies, chopped,
or 1 dried cascabel chili, soaked (see
page 11), flesh scooped out, and puréed
1-inch piece fresh gingerroot,
peeled and chopped

1/2 pound shelled peanuts (about 1
1/2 cups), toasted (see page 14) and crushed
2/3 cup water
Juice of 1 lime
Salt and freshly ground black pepper
1 teaspoon five-spice powder

Heat the oil in a heavy pan over medium heat and sauté the chilies and gingerroot for 2 minutes. Add the peanuts and water and cook for a further 3-4 minutes. Then add the lime juice. Season with salt and pepper, and stir in the five-spice powder.

BLACK OLIVE AND CHILI SAUCE
MEDIUM-HOT

A strong-tasting sauce that enhances the flavor of fried zucchini, stir-fried eggplant, and toasted goat cheese.

1 red bell pepper, quartered
1-2 fresh medium–hot red chilies, halved
and seeded, or 1 dried ancho or
chipotle chili, soaked (see page 11)

2 tablespoons black olive paste, from a jar
1/4 cup olive oil
1 tablespoon balsamic vineger
Salt and freshly ground black pepper

Place the red bell pepper and chilies under a hot broiler, skin side up, and cook until the skins blister and turn black, then transfer to a food processor. Add the rest of the ingredients and blend until smooth.

Season to taste with salt and pepper.

AIOLI MEDIUM-HOT

This popular sauce has a wonderful garlicky flavor. Try it with raw vegetables, grilled shrimp, or asparagus, or use to flavor fish soup.

5 cloves garlic, peeled
1/2 teaspoon salt
2 egg yolks

Juice of 1/2 lemon
3/4–1 cup olive oil
Salt and freshly ground black pepper

Put the garlic and salt in a mortar and crush to a paste with a pestle. Turn into a food processor and add the egg yolks and lemon juice. Blend for 1 minute.

With the motor still running, slowly pour in the oil—too much too quickly will make the sauce curdle—until the mixture thickens.

Season to taste with salt and pepper.

CILANTRO PISTOU SAUCE MILD

This sauce has a strongly aromatic flavor. Serve with goat cheese, stir into vegetable soup, or toss with pasta.

1/3 cup chopped fresh cilantro
5 cloves garlic, peeled
5-6 tablespoons olive oil

Juice of 1/2 lemon
1/4 teaspoon salt
1/4 teaspoon freshly ground black pepper

Put all the ingredients in a food processor and blend until smooth.

HOT TOMATO AND CHILI SAUCE HOT

This is mighty hot! Try this full-flavored sauce with grilled zucchini, over globe artichokes, or with seafood or focaccia bread.

3 tablespoons sun-dried tomato paste
2 fresh hot red chilies, or 1 dried habañero chili, soaked (see page 11)
2 tablespoons olive oil

Juice of 1/2 lemon
2 tablespoons red wine vinegar
Salt and freshly ground black pepper

Put all the ingredients in the food processor and blend until smooth.

Season to taste with salt and pepper.

AROMATIC YOGURT RAITA COOL

Use this fresh, minty sauce to cool down curries, dhals, or any hot dish.

3 tablespoons minced fresh mint
1/4 teaspoon salt

1/4 teaspoon freshly ground black pepper
2/3 cup plain yogurt

Put all the ingredients in a bowl and mix together until smooth.

SPICED LEMON DRESSING SPICY

This fresh, tangy sauce is perfection with asparagus, shrimp, and cold chicken.

2 lemons, peeled segments and grated rind
1-inch piece fresh gingerroot, peeled

2/3 cup sunflower oil
Salt and freshly ground black pepper

Put all the ingredients in a food processor and blend until smooth.

Season to taste with salt and pepper.

HORSERADISH CREAM MEDIUM-HOT

This is a hot sauce with a smooth, creamy texture. Delicious with beets, new potatoes, smoked salmon, peppered mackerel, or cold beef.

2/3 cup whipping cream
2- to 3-inch piece fresh horseradish (about 5 ounces), peeled and grated
Pinch of grated lemon rind

1 teaspoon lemon juice
1 teaspoon Dijon mustard
1 tablespoon chopped fresh chives
Salt and freshly ground black pepper

Whip the cream until thick, then stir in the rest of the ingredients and mix together well.

Season to taste with salt and pepper.

CHILI-PEPPER SHERRY HOT

Quick and easy to make, chili-pepper sherry will definitely spike up any vegetable soup, broth, or consommé. Excellent in stews, tomato juice, and Bloody Marys.

2 1/2 cups dry sherry

1 fresh hot green chili, or 5 dried bird's eye chilies

Put the sherry and chili in a clean bottle and leave to steep for 1 week.

Top up with more sherry and use sparingly.

• Chili-pepper sherry will keep for at least a year.

CHILI OIL HOT

Hot chili oil is simple to make and just the thing to liven up plain mayonnaise and salad dressings.

Small bottle extra virgin olive oil

12 small fresh hot red and green chilies, scored all over with the tip of a knife, or 12 dried bird's eye chilies

Put the oil and chilies in a sterilized bottle and set aside to let the chilies infuse into the oil for 2 weeks. Use sparingly.

• Keep in a cool place, away from the light.

HOT MUSTARD AND HORSERADISH SAUCE HOT

Don't be under any illusion—this sauce is hot. Excellent with smoked fish or any raw fish or meat tartare.

3-inch piece fresh horseradish, peeled and grated (about 1/4 cup)
1 dill pickle, about 3 inches long
1 tablespoon capers

1 teaspoon mustard powder
1/2 teaspoon freshly ground black pepper
3-4 tablespoons thick cream or fromage blanc
Juice of 1 lemon

Put all the ingredients, except the cream and lemon juice, in a food procesor and blend until very fine. Transfer the mixture to a bowl and lightly stir in the cream and lemon juice—do not overstir or the sauce will curdle.

Right: Hot Pepper Vinaigrette

CUCUMBER AND GINGER SAUCE MEDIUM

This sauce has a lovely Asian flavor and is delicious with grilled swordfish, eel, monkfish, and salmon.

2 cloves garlic, peeled and minced
2 fresh medium-hot green chilies, minced,
or 2 dried pasado chilies, soaked
(see page 11) and minced
2-inch piece fresh gingerroot,
peeled and chopped

4-inch piece English hothouse cucumber,
chopped
⁷/₈ cup rice vinegar
¹/₄ cup soy sauce
¹/₂ cup sesame seeds, toasted (see page 14)

Put all the ingredients in a bowl and mix together well.

RED-CHILI VELOUTE MEDIUM

This sauce is wonderful with clams and mussels. Alternatively, serve it with smoked haddock (or other smoked fish).

2 tablespoons olive oil or butter
2 cloves garlic, peeled and minced
1 fresh medium-hot red chili, minced,
or 1 dried ancho chili, soaked
(see page 11) and minced

2 wineglasses white wine
4 green onions, trimmed and chopped
3 heaped tablespoons crème fraîche
Salt and freshly ground black pepper
2 tablespoons chopped fresh flat-leaf parsley

Heat the oil or butter in a heavy pan and gently sauté the garlic and chili. Add the white wine, bring to a boil, and simmer for 3-4 minutes.

Stir in the green onions and cream and simmer for a further 1-2 minutes, then season and sprinkle with parsley.

• For a lovely smoky flavor, use 2-3 dried chipotle chilies, soaked (see page 11) and puréed.

• To make a wonderful soup, pour the sauce into a deep-sided pan, add 2 wineglasses of white wine, and bring to a boil. Throw in 2 ¹/₂ pounds of well-scrubbed mussels, put on the lid, and cook until the mussels are all open, about 5 minutes.

MALAYSIAN PICKLE SAUCE HOT

This sauce has a slightly crunchy texture and is excellent with raw or grilled fish, plus shrimp and chicken.

¹/₂ turnip, grated
¹/₂ parsnip, grated
1 carrot, grated
3 tablespoons rice vinegar
Juice of 1 lime
2 teaspoons soy sauce
1 tablespoon sesame seeds,
toasted (see page 14)

1 heaped tablespoon peanuts, toasted
(see page 14) and crushed in a food
processor or coffee grinder
1 fresh hot red chili, sliced and seeded, or
1 dried chipotle chili, soaked
(see page 11) and chopped
Salt and freshly ground black pepper

Put all the ingredients into a bowl and mix together well.

Season to taste with salt and pepper.

Right: New Orleans Red-Bean Sauce

SCALLION SAUCE MEDIUM

Quick and easy to prepare, this sophisticated sauce is delicious with fishcakes and grilled white fish.

1 cup homemade or good-quality
bottled mayonnaise
3 tablespoons whipping cream
1-2 teaspoons Tabasco sauce
Juice of 1/2 lemon
1/4 teaspoon mustard powder
1 teaspoon salt

Freshly ground pepper
1/4 teaspoon sugar
1/2 cup trimmed and roughly
chopped scallions
1 hard-boiled egg, chopped
1 heaped tablespoon chopped fresh parsley
1 teaspoon Worcestershire sauce

Put all the ingredients into a large bowl and mix together well.

CREAMY PEPPER SAUCE MEDIUM

This colorful sauce not only looks good but tastes wonderful, too. Try it with fishcakes, crab cakes, or grilled goat cheese served on a bed of lettuce.

1 tablespoon olive oil
1 tablespoon butter
3 red or yellow bell peppers, roughly chopped
3 cloves garlic, peeled and crushed
2 teaspoons ground coriander

1/2 teaspoon cayenne
1/4 cup crème fraîche
Salt and freshly ground black pepper
3 scallions, minced

Heat the oil and butter in a heavy-based pan over a low heat and gently sauté the bell peppers and garlic until soft. Add the coriander, cayenne, crème fraîche, and seasoning and stir well.

Put the mixture in a food processor and blend until smooth, then transfer to a bowl and sprinkle with the green onions.

AROMATIC FENNEL SAUCE SPICY

Simple to make, try this delicate, creamy sauce with a firm white fish such as sea bass, sole, or turbot.

1 tablespoon butter
1 tablespoon sunflower oil
1 fennel bulb, roughly chopped
3 tablespoons Pernod
1/2 teaspoon caraway seeds

6 fennel seeds
1 teaspoon cumin seeds
1 1/4 cup crème fraîche
Salt and freshly ground black pepper
2 tablespoons chopped fresh flat-leaf parsley

Melt the butter with the oil in a heavy pan over a low heat and gently sauté the fennel until soft but not brown.

Add the Pernod, then turn up the heat and stir in the caraway, fennel, and cumin seeds. Simmer until half the liquid has evaporated, then add the cream, bring to a boil, and season to taste with salt and pepper.

Transfer the mixture to a food processor and blend until smooth.

Sprinkle with parsley.

GREEN CHUTNEY SAUCE MEDIUM-HOT

A slightly sweet, piquant sauce. Wonderful with red mullet, grey mullet, or any Pacific fish.

3 tablespoons oil
1 teaspoon black mustard seeds
3 cloves garlic, peeled
2-inch piece fresh gingerroot, peeled
2 fresh medium-hot green chilies, or 1 dried
habañero chili, soaked (see page 11)
2 tablespoons water

2 mangoes, flesh diced into 1/2-inch cubes
2 tablespoons sherry
Juice of 1 lime
1 tablespoon sugar
2 tablespoons chopped fresh cilantro
Salt and freshly ground black pepper

Heat the oil in a heavy pan over medium heat and cook the mustard seeds until they begin to "pop." Remove the pan from the heat and set aside.

Put the garlic, gingerroot, chilies, and water in a food processor and blend until a smooth paste is formed. Transfer the paste to the pan and cook over a low heat for 5 minutes.

Stir in the mango cubes, sherry, lime juice, and sugar and slowly heat through.

Sprinkle with the cilantro, season with salt and pepper, and serve.

SPICED YOGURT SAUCE COOL

A spicy yet cooling sauce for marinated fish or curry dishes. Alternatively, use as a dipping sauce for grilled shrimp.

2 tablespoons sunflower oil
4 cloves garlic, peeled and chopped
1 teaspoon turmeric
1 teaspoon ground cinnamon
1 teaspoon cumin seeds
1 teaspoon fennel seeds

1/2 teaspoon cayenne
1/2 teaspoon freshly ground black pepper
10 cardamom pods
1/2 cup thick plain yogurt
Salt and freshly ground black pepper

Put the oil in a heavy pan, add the garlic, turmeric, cinnamon, cumin seeds, fennel seeds, cayenne, black pepper, and cardamom pods and gently heat them for 2-3 minutes.

Transfer the mixture to a food processor and blend until smooth, then return to the pan. Add the yogurt and gently heat through.

Press the mixture through a strainer to remove spice husks, then stir thoroughly.

Season with salt and pepper and serve.

• This sauce makes an excellent marinade. Use exactly the same method but don't reheat with the yogurt.

SWEET AND SOUR PEACH SAUCE MILD

As the name suggests this is a wonderful combination of sweet and sour ingredients. Excellent with lobster, ham, or red mullet.

2 tablespoons rice vinegar
2 tablespoons honey
3 ripe peaches, pitted and finely sliced
1 fresh mild red chili, minced, or 1 dried

ancho chili, soaked (see page 11) and minced
1/2 red onion, minced
Salt and freshly ground black pepper

Put all the ingredients in a bowl and mix together well. Season to taste with salt and pepper.

• Will keep for a week in the refrigerator.

JAFFA SAUCE MILD

An ingenious combination of ingredients, specially created to complement Pacific fish such as tuna, swordfish, barracuda, and parrot fish.

1 tablespoon olive oil
Rind of 1 orange, grated or cut into fine strips
Juice of 2 oranges
1/2 English hothouse cucumber, peeled, seeded, and minced

3 shallots, finely sliced
1/2 teaspoon poppy seeds
2 tablespoons chopped fresh cilantro
Salt and freshly ground black pepper

Put all the ingredients into a bowl and mix together well.
Season to taste with salt and pepper.

MOROCCAN BLACK-PEPPER SAUCE

HOT AND AROMATIC

This strong, gutsy sauce is based on a well-known Middle Eastern recipe. Delicious with grilled or steamed white fish such as halibut, monkfish, sea bass, or cod, as well as large shrimp and sea scallops. It also makes a good dipping sauce.

4 tablespoons butter or sunflower oil
2 onions, minced or grated
1/3 cup minced fresh parsley
2 teaspoons freshly ground black pepper

1/2 teaspoon cayenne
2 teaspoons ground cinnamon
2 1/2 cups thick plain yogurt
Pinch of salt

Heat the butter or oil in a heavy-based pan, add the onions, parsley, black pepper, cayenne, and cinnamon and gently sauté for 2-3 minutes, taking care not to burn them.

Stir in the yogurt and salt, then quickly remove the pan from the heat.

SPICED CUCUMBER SAUCE MILD

Based on an Indian recipe, this tasty sauce is delicious with fish such as barbecued or marinated tuna, grilled swordfish, or shrimp.
It also makes an excellent cooler for curries and other hot dishes.

1/2 English hothouse cucumber, seeded, and minced
1/4 melon, skin removed, seeded, and minced
1 teaspoon ground coriander

1 tablespoon chopped fresh mint
2 cloves garlic, peeled, and minced
Salt and freshly ground black pepper
3 tablespoons olive oil
Juice of 1/2 lemon

Put all the ingredients into a bowl and mix thoroughly.

PARSLEY AND LEMON SAUCE MILD

Use this light, herbal sauce to stuff sardines or rolled flounder or sole *en papillote*, or serve it with steamed or grilled cod.

1 cup minced fresh flat-leaf parsley
1 teaspoon ground white pepper
1/2 teaspoon salt

1/3 cup sunflower oil
2 tablespoons olive oil
Grated rind and juice of 1 lemon

Combine the parsley, pepper, and salt in the food processor.
Switch on the motor and slowly pour the oils into the mixture.
Add the lemon rind and juice, then check the seasoning and serve.

CILANTRO AND GARLIC SAUCE

MILD AND AROMATIC

Bursting with flavor, this wonderfully aromatic sauce is perfection with grilled shrimp, mussels, clams, squid, or a mixed seafood salad.

2 tablespoons sunflower oil
2 tablespoons walnut or hazelnut oil
2 tablespoons lime juice
2 heaped tablespoons chopped fresh cilantro

4 cloves garlic, peeled
1 teaspoon freshly ground black pepper
Salt
2 tablespoons cream

Put all the ingredients into a food processor and blend until smooth.

Right: Lemon and Chili Marinade

CARDAMOM SAUCE MEDIUM-HOT

This strong, spicy sauce complements grilled chicken breasts and lamb chops to perfection.

3 tablespoons sunflower oil
1-inch piece fresh gingerroot,
peeled and chopped
4 cloves garlic, peeled and minced
1 teaspoon cardamom pods

1 teaspoon fennel seeds
1 teaspoon ground coriander
1 1/4 cups plain yogurt
Salt

Put all the ingredients, except the yogurt, in a food processor and blend to a coarse paste. Transfer to a heavy pan and gently warm through. Stir in the yogurt and bring to a boil. Season with salt and serve.

• Try cooking small pieces of raw chicken or lamb in the sauce: Simmer until the meat is tender, 30-40 minutes. (Use milk instead of yogurt, if preferred.)

CILANTRO AND HONEY SAUCE MILD AND SPICY

The unusual combination of honey, cilantro, and citrus fruits is sweet and fresh. Serve over chicken breasts or roast duck.

2 tablespoons butter
1-inch piece fresh gingerroot,
peeled and cut in thin slices
1 teaspoon grated lemon rind
1 teaspoon grated orange rind
1/2 teaspoon ground cloves

1/2 teaspoon caraway seeds
6 cardamom pods
Juice of 1 orange
6 tablespoons honey
3 tablespoons minced fresh cilantro
Salt and freshly ground black pepper

Melt the butter in a heavy pan over medium heat. Add the gingerroot, lemon rind, orange rind, cloves, caraway seeds, and cardamom pods and heat for 2-3 minutes, taking care not to burn them.

Stir in the orange juice and honey, then bring to a boil and simmer for 2 minutes.

Sprinkle with cilantro, season with salt and pepper and serve.

HOT CHILI AND COCONUT SAUCE HOT

This is an inspired combination of mouthwatering ingredients, especially for lovers of hot food. Excellent with chicken and fish.

4 ounces unsweetened coconut cream
2/3 cup boiling water
6 fresh green Thai chilies, seeded and minced,
or 5 dried tepin chilies, crushed, or 2 dried
habañero chilies, soaked (see page 11)
and minced
2 tablespoons chopped fresh cilantro
1 tablespoon ground cumin
1-inch piece fresh gingerroot, peeled
and chopped
1 onion, minced

3 cloves garlic, peeled
1 teaspoon freshly ground black pepper
Grated rind of 1/2 lemon
1 tablespoon fresh lime juice
2 stems lemon grass, tough outer
leaves removed
1 teaspoon coriander seeds, crushed
1 tablespoon peanut oil
1 1/2 cups hot water
1 lime, sliced

Whisking with a fork, dissolve the coconut cream in the boiling water. Set aside to cool.

Put the remaining ingredients, except the lime slices, in the food processor and blend until smooth, then transfer the mixture to a bowl and stir in the coconut cream.

Garnish with slices of lime.

ANDALUSIAN SAUCE MEDIUM-HOT

This is a fairly robust sauce. Serve with ham, corned beef, pork, or chicken breasts.

4 cloves garlic, peeled and chopped
1 red onion, quartered
1 fresh medium-hot red chili, or 1 dried
guindilla chili, soaked, puréed, and
sieved (see page 11)
1/3 cup chopped fresh mint
3 tablespoons olive oil

1/2 pound smoked ham, chopped into
small pieces
1 can (16-ounce) green lentils,
with the juice
Pinch of saffron threads
2/3 cup water
Salt and freshly ground black pepper

Combine the garlic, onion, chili, and mint in a food processor and blend until fine.

Heat the oil in a wok or deep-sided pan and stir-fry the processed mixture with the ham for 1-2 minutes.

Add the lentils, saffron, salt, and water (add a little more water if the sauce is too dry) and simmer for 5-6 minutes.

Season to taste with salt and pepper.

• To make a richly flavored soup, add 2 1/2 cups of good stock.

Right: Green Chutney Sauce

Above: Sweet and Sour Peach Sauce

Pineapple and Macadamia Sauce
MILD

This is a tangy, full-bodied sauce with a sweet, spicy flavor. Try it with barbecued marinated chicken.

1 1/2 cups canned or fresh, ripe pineapple, drained and crushed
1 stem lemon grass, tough outer leaves removed
1 clove garlic, peeled
6 shallots, roughly chopped
2-3 dried chipotle chilies, soaked (see page 11)
1 cup unsalted macadamia nuts
2 tablespoons peanut oil
1 cup canned unsweetened coconut milk
1 heaped tablespoon tamarind pulp, soaked in water, then drained and pressed through a strainer
2 heaped tablespoons unsalted cashew nuts, toasted (see page 14)
1 teaspoon brown sugar
1 tablespoon soy sauce
Salt and freshly ground black pepper

Place the crushed pineapple in a bowl and set aside.

Put the lemon grass, garlic, shallots, chilies, and macadamia nuts in the food processor and blend until a smooth paste is formed, 1-2 minutes.

Heat the oil in a heavy saucepan and fry the paste for 3-4 minutes, stirring constantly.

Add the coconut milk and bring to a boil, then simmer for 30 seconds, stirring all the time.

Add the remaining ingredients and simmer for a further 5 minutes. Put the mixture into a bowl and let cool at room temperature.

Season with salt and pepper and stir in the pineapple just before serving.

Tomato Catsup MILD

This is the real thing. Use this tasty sauce to pep up barbecued or chargrilled chicken, burgers and beef hash.

1 tablespoon olive oil
1 large onion, minced
6 very ripe tomatoes, seeded and roughly chopped, or 1 can (16-ounce) crushed Italian tomatoes
1/4 cup packed brown sugar or light molasses
2 tablespoons white sugar
1 teaspoon salt
1/2 teaspoon black pepper
1/4 teaspoon ground allspice
1/4 cup malt or cider vinegar
1 tablespoon tomato paste
Juice of 1/2 lemon
Salt and freshly ground black pepper

Heat the oil in a deep-sided pan and, when it begins to smoke, add the onion and tomatoes and cover. Let the tomatoes bubble furiously. When they calm down, remove the lid and add the rest of the ingredients, except the lemon juice.

Lower the heat and cook uncovered for 30 minutes, stirring occasionally. Add a little water if the liquid evaporates too much during the cooking process.

Remove the pan from the heat and add the lemon juice, then transfer the mixture to a food processor and blend until smooth.

Season to taste with salt and pepper.

• For best results, press the catsup through a strainer after blending.

Thai Red Curry Sauce HOT

Red and green Thai sauces can be used to flavor or accompany a wide variety of dishes and ingredients. Serve over beef, chicken, shrimp, monkfish, or vegetables. Alternatively, use as a side sauce for grilled chicken. (See also Thai Green Curry Sauce.)

1 tablespoon sunflower oil
2 tablespoons red curry paste
1 can (14-ounce) unsweetened coconut milk
4-8 baby eggplants, whole or halved depending on their size

Heat the oil in a heavy pan and gently fry the curry paste for 1-2 minutes. Then add the coconut milk and eggplants and simmer for 10-15 minutes.

Thai Green Curry Sauce HOT

Thai Green Curry Sauce has a slightly sour taste, which complements vegetables, beef, chicken, and shrimp to perfection.

1 tablespoon sunflower oil
2 tablespoons green curry paste
1 can (14-ounce) unsweetened coconut milk
4-8 baby eggplants, whole or halved depending on their size

Heat the oil in a heavy pan and gently fry the paste for 1-2 minutes. Then add the coconut milk and eggplants and simmer for 10-15 minutes.

• Cook thin strips of beef, small pieces of chicken, shrimp, or vegetables in the sauce.

Spiced quince sauce MILD

The sweet and sour combination of quince and chilies makes this an ideal sauce to serve with roast partridge, roast pork, or duck breasts.

1 stalk celery, finely diced

3 ripe quinces or pears, peeled, cored, and finely diced

1 fresh mild green chili, finely diced, or 1 dried pasado chili, soaked (see page 11) and finely diced

2 cloves garlic, peeled and minced

1 tablespoon honey

2 tablespoons white wine vinegar

1 tablespoon lemon juice

Salt

Put all the ingredients in a pan, then bring to a boil and simmer for 1 minute.

Transfer the mixture to a bowl and stir well.

• This sauce can be served hot or cold.

Peppered parsley sauce MEDIUM

This fresh, highly seasoned sauce is excellent with roast beef, ham, cod steaks, and monkfish.

1 cup chopped fresh parsley

Grated rind of 1 lemon

Juice of 2 lemons

1 small onion, quartered

6 tablespoons olive oil

1 tablespoon mustard powder

1 tablespoon capers

1 dill pickle, about 3 inches long

1/2 teaspoon freshly ground black pepper

1/2 teaspoon cayenne

Salt

Put all the ingredients in a food processor and blend until smooth.

Season with salt to taste.

Sweet pickle sauce MEDIUM

The sharp, slightly tangy flavor of this delicious sauce works well with baked ham, pork sausages, blood sausage, and cheese.

1 1/4 cups water

2 1/2 cups malt or cider vinegar

Pinch of salt

1 cup cauliflower florets

10 pearl onions

1/2 green bell pepper, cut into 1/4-inch dice

1 dill pickle, chopped

1 teaspoon yellow mustard seeds

1 teaspoon green peppercorns in brine, drained and slightly crushed

1 tablespooon mustard powder

1 tablespooon sunflower oil

1 tablespoon sugar

Salt and freshly ground black pepper

Put the water, vinegar, and salt in a pan and bring to a boil. Add the cauliflower, pearl onions, and green bell pepper and cook for 5 minutes, then drain, retaining 1/3 cup of the cooking liquid.

Put the remaining ingredients in a bowl, add the reserved liquid and cooked vegetables, and mix together well. Season to taste with salt and pepper.

Black-bean sauce VERY HOT

This powerful sauce is not for the faint-hearted! Excellent with beef hash or burgers.

2-3 tablespoons sunflower oil

2 fresh habañero chilies, or 3 dried habañero chilies, soaked (see page 11)

4 cloves garlic, peeled

4 tomatoes, seeded and chopped

1 can (16-ounce) black beans, drained, or 1 1/3 cups dried black beans, soaked in water overnight, then drained and cooked until soft but not mushy, or 1 can (16-ounce) black beans, drained

1/4 cup chopped fresh cilantro

Salt and freshly ground black pepper

Put the oil, chilies, and garlic in a food processor and blend until smooth.

Transfer the mixture to a heavy pan, add the tomatoes, and cook over medium heat for 3 minutes.

Add the beans and cook for a further 3 minutes.

Stir in the cilantro, season with salt and pepper and serve.

Spice Island Sauce MEDIUM-HOT

As its name suggests, this sauce has a pungent, spicy flavor.
Delicious with blackeyed peas or borlotti beans. Alternatively, try it
with polenta.

4 thick slices Canadian bacon, rind removed
4 cloves garlic, peeled
1/2 white onion
2 fresh medium-hot red chilies, or 1 dried
cascabel chili, soaked (see page 11)
1 teaspoon dried marjoram
1 teaspoon medium curry powder
1/2 teaspoon fennel seeds

1 tablespoon green peppercorns in brine,
drained and slightly crushed
1 cup sun-dried tomatoes packed in oil,
drained
6 fresh tomatoes, chopped, or 1 can
(16-ounce) crushed Italian tomatoes
Salt and freshly ground black pepper

Put all the ingredients, except the fresh tomatoes, in a food processor
and blend until fine, then transfer the mixture to a heavy pan. Sauté
for 4-5 minutes.

Add the fresh tomatoes and simmer for a further 10 minutes. Season
and serve.

Green-Peppercorn Sauce

MEDIUM AND SPICY

This is a sophisticated sauce with an unusual texture. Serve over
roasted duck breasts, medallions of veal, or filet mignon.

1 1/2 tablespoons butter
1 1/2 tablespoons sugar
2 apples, peeled, cored, and cut into 8
segments each
1/4 cup white vermouth

3/4 cup homemade vegetable or poultry stock
2-3 tablespoons whipping cream
1 1/2 tablespoons green peppercorns in brine,
drained and crushed
Salt and freshly ground black pepper

Melt the butter and sugar in a heavy pan over medium heat and sauté
the apple segments for 2-3 minutes.

Using a slotted spoon, transfer the apples to a bowl and and set aside.

Add the vermouth and stock to the pan and simmer until the mixture
reduces a little, 3-4 minutes. Then add the cream and cook for 3-4
minutes longer.

Return the apples to the pan, add the peppercorns, and stir together
well. Season to taste with salt and pepper.

Sweet and Sour Sesame Sauce MILD

Sweet yet sour, with a lovely crunchy texture, this is an ideal sauce to
serve with crisp roasted duck or grilled chicken, or as a dish on
the side.

3 tablespoons red currant jelly
2 tablespoons soy sauce
2/3 cup water
1 teaspoon minced fresh gingerroot
1 small fresh mild red chili, minced

1/2 English hothouse cucumber, peeled,
seeded, and chopped
4 scallions, sliced
1 tablespoon sesame seeds,
toasted (see page 14)

Put the red currant jelly, soy sauce, water, gingerroot, and chili in a
saucepan and bring to a boil, then lower the heat and simmer for 5
minutes, stirring occasionally.

Add the cucumber, scallions, and sesame seeds and stir thoroughly.
Remove from the heat and serve.

Chili Aioli HOT

Excellent with crudités, grilled fish, shrimp, and lamb kebabs.

3 (or more) fresh hot red chilies, or 2
tablespoons Pimenton de la Vera chili powder
3 cloves garlic, peeled
1/2 teaspoon freshly ground black pepper
3 egg yolks

7/8 cup olive oil, or 1/2 cup olive oil and
6 tablespoons sunflower oil
Juice of 1/2 lemon
Salt and freshly ground black pepper.

Put the chilies (or chili powder) and garlic into a food processor and
blend for 30 seconds, then add the black pepper and egg yolks.

With the motor still running, slowly pour in three-quarters of the oil,
then turn off the processor, add a teaspoon of lemon juice, and taste.
Keep adding the lemon juice, a teaspoon at a time, until the desired
sharpness is acquired, then slowly pour in the rest of the oil.

Season to taste with salt and pepper.

Right: Black-Bean Sauce

SHERRY AND GARLIC SAUCE AROMATIC

This rich, warm sauce is the perfect accompaniment to homemade meatballs. Alternatively, try it with pan-fried chicken or pork chops.

1 fresh medium-hot green chili, roughly chopped, or 1 dried guajillo chili, soaked (see page 11) and roughly chopped
2 cloves garlic, peeled and roughly chopped
1 thick slice bacon, cut in pieces

1 wineglass dry sherry
3 tablespoons crème fraîche
2-3 saffron threads
Salt and freshly ground black pepper
1 heaped tablespoon chopped fresh mint

Put the chili, garlic, and bacon in the food processor and process to minced.

Transfer the minced mixture to a heavy pan and sauté over medium heat for 2-3 minutes, then add the sherry and bring to a boil. Simmer for 1-2 minutes. Add the crème fraîche and saffron and simmer for a further 2 minutes.

Season with salt and pepper and sprinkle with mint.

NEAPOLITAN SWEET-PEPPER SAUCE

MEDIUM-HOT

Bursting with Mediterranean flavors and aromas, this wonderful sauce is delicious with burgers, meat pâtés, sausages, and meat loaves.

2 tablespoons olive oil
4 thick slices bacon or pancetta, roughly chopped
1 red onion, quartered
4 cloves garlic, peeled
1 fresh hot green chili, or 2 dried guajillo chilies, soaked, puréed, and sieved (see page 11)

2 red bell peppers, roughly chopped
3 tomatoes, quartered
1 wineglass white wine
1 tablespoon chopped fresh parsley
Salt and freshly ground black pepper

Put the oil, bacon, onion, garlic, and green chili in a food processor and blend until minced.

Transfer the mixture to a heavy pan, and cook over medium heat for 2-3 minutes. (Discard excess fat, if desired.)

Add the red bell peppers, tomatoes, and wine and simmer for 10 minutes.

Stir in the parsley and season to taste with salt and pepper.

Left: Green-Peppercorn Sauce

DIPS

All recipes are for four portions.

LIME-PICKLE DIP HOT

This combination of hot pickle, yogurt, and cilantro is highly recommended. Serve with cheese, ham, vegetables, or skewered grilled chicken.

3/4 cup hot lime pickle
(available from Indian markets)

1 1/4 cups thick plain yogurt
1 heaped tablespoon chopped fresh cilantro

Put all the ingredients in a food processor and blend until smooth.

• If a sweeter taste is preferred, add 1 teaspoon brown sugar.

CILANTRO AND YOGURT DIP MEDIUM-HOT

Thick and creamy, fresh-tasting, and smooth, this pungent green dip is excellent with fish and grilled chicken, and is just the thing to perk up a plain baked potato.

1 teaspoon cumin seeds, toasted (see page 14)
1 1/2 tablespoons water
1/2 cup chopped fresh cilantro
Juice of 1/2 lemon

1 teaspoon salt
1 cup thick plain yogurt
2 fresh hot green chilies, seeded and minced
Freshly ground black pepper

Put the cumin seeds in a blender and grind for 1 minute. Add the water, cilantro, and lemon juice and blend again until a smooth paste is formed (scrape the mixture down the side of the bowl if it sticks).

Mix the remaining ingredients in a bowl, stir in the paste, and mix thoroughly.

• Will keep in the refrigerator for 2 days.

SESAME AND GINGER DIP MEDIUM

This ambrosial combination not only smells good but tastes wonderful, too. Perfection with spring rolls, deep-fried shrimp, or wonton.

1 tablespoon cashew nuts, toasted
(see page 14)
2 cloves garlic, peeled and minced
1 tablespoon sugar
2 1/2-inch piece fresh gingerroot,
peeled and minced
1 tablespoon soy sauce

1 tablespoon sesame oil
1 tablespoon tomato paste
1 tablespoon rice vinegar
1 teaspoon chili oil
1 teaspoon mustard powder
1 1/2 tablespoons sesame seeds,
toasted (see page 14)

Put the nuts, garlic, sugar, and gingerroot in a food processor and blend until smooth. Transfer the mixture to a bowl and add the soy sauce, sesame oil, tomato paste, vinegar, chili oil, and mustard. Mix together well. Stir in the sesame seeds just before serving.

GUACAMOLE MEDIUM

This all-time favorite from Mexico can be served as a dish on its own, with tortilla chips.

1 onion, minced
1 stalk celery, chopped
2 tomatoes, seeded and chopped
3 fresh green jalapeño chilies, minced, or
2 dried pasado chilies, soaked
(see page 11) and minced
2 tablespoons chopped fresh cilantro

1/2 teaspoon salt
1/2-1 teaspoon cayenne
1 tablespoon lime juice
Freshly ground black pepper
Flesh of 2 ripe avocados, prepared at the
last minute

Put all the ingredients, except the avocado flesh, in a food processor and blend for 30 seconds or until coarse-fine but not mushy. Transfer the mixture to a bowl.

In a separate bowl roughly mash the avocado flesh, then add to the chili mixture and season to taste.

• Cover tightly with plastic wrap and keep in the refrigerator.

• If you make this dip in advance, the surface may discolor. If it does, scrape off the affected layer—it will not alter the taste.

Right: Sesame and Ginger Dip

ROASTED EGGPLANT DIP SPICY

This lovely, creamy dip has a delicate flavor, which complements skewered lamb, grilled sea scallops, or celery sticks beautifully. Alternatively, serve over grilled goat cheese.

Preheat the oven to 475°F.

3 medium-sized eggplants
1 tablespoon sunflower oil
2-3 cloves garlic, peeled and minced
1 fresh green jalapeño chili, seeded and minced, or 1 dried chipotle chili, soaked (see page 11) and minced

Grated rind and juice of 1 lemon
2 heaped tablespoons chopped fresh mint
2 heaped tablespoons chopped fresh cilantro
1/4 cup thick plain yogurt
Salt and freshly ground black pepper

Put the eggplants in a small baking pan and cook in the oven for 1 hour or until soft; remove from the oven. Split the eggplants down the center, remove the central seeds, and discard. Scoop the remaining flesh out of the skins and set aside. Discard the skins.

Heat the oil in a heavy pan over medium heat and cook the garlic and chili for 1-2 minutes. Pour the cooked ingredients, including the oil, into a food processor and add the lemon rind and juice. Blend to a paste. Add the eggplant flesh, mint, cilantro, and yogurt and blend until smooth.

Season to taste with salt and pepper.

PEANUT DIP MEDIUM

The perfect accompaniment for satay chicken, beef, and lamb.

2 tablespoons sesame oil
2 cloves garlic, peeled and minced
2 fresh green jalapeño chilies, minced, or 5 dried tepin chilies, crushed
2 stems lemon grass, outer leaves removed, minced

1 cup crunchy peanut butter
1 cup canned unsweetened coconut milk
1 heaped tablespoon chopped fresh cilantro
Juice of 2 limes
Sea salt and freshly ground black pepper

Heat the oil in a heavy pan and gently sauté the garlic, chilies, and lemon grass for 1 minute.

Remove the pan from the heat and add the peanut butter and coconut milk. Simmer over a low heat for 4-5 minutes, then stir in the remaining ingredients and season to taste with salt and pepper.

• Let the dip stand for at least 2 hours before serving.

FRESH HERB DIP MILD AND AROMATIC

As its name suggests, this tasty dip has a fresh, rather spicy taste. Excellent with hard-boiled quail eggs, raw vegetables, or shrimp.

1 teaspoon cumin seeds
1 teaspoon fennel seeds
1/2 teaspoon black mustard seeds
1/4 cup chopped fresh basil
1/4 cup chopped fresh chives

1/4 cup chopped fresh parsley
2 cloves garlic, peeled and minced
2 tablespoons extra virgin olive oil
1 1/4 cups thick plain yogurt
Salt and freshly ground black pepper

Toast the cumin seeds, fennel seeds, and mustard seeds (see page 14).

Put all the ingredients into a food processor and blend until smooth.

Season to taste with salt and pepper.

CURRIED PINEAPPLE DIP MEDIUM

This colorful dip is bound to impress. Serve with raw vegetables, chicken on sticks, pitta bread, or crackers.

1/2 small pineapple, peeled, cored, and chopped
1/3 cup thick plain yogurt
1 teaspoon medium curry powder
1/2 teaspoon turmeric

2/3 cup crème fraîche
1 stalk celery, minced
1 fresh green jalapeño chili, minced, or 1/2 dried habañero chili, soaked (see page 11) and minced

Put the pineapple in a strainer or colander. Using your fists, squeeze it against the sides to extract the juice—this will prevent the dip from curdling or becoming too runny. Discard the juice and chop the pineapple into very small pieces.

Place all the ingredients into a bowl and mix together well.

AILLADE HOT

A wonderful hot, crunchy, garlicky dip. Serve with raw vegetables, grilled shrimp, or cold cuts.

2-3 large cloves garlic, peeled and minced
2 tablespoons minced walnut pieces
1/2 teaspoon salt
2 tablespoons chopped fresh parsley

2 teaspoons white wine vinegar
1/4 cup walnut oil
1 egg yolk

Put the garlic, walnuts, salt, parsley, and vinegar into a bowl and mix together well. Slowly add the oil, 1 tablespoon at a time, stirring constantly.

Add the egg yolk and beat vigorously for a few seconds to emulsify.

• Try pine nuts instead of walnut pieces.

• For extra zing, add 1 tablespoon chopped fresh chives.

• This will keep in the refrigerator for 4 days.

SALSAS

'Salsa' is the Mexican word for sauce. Salsas can be fiery hot, mild, or exotically flavored, and are made from a combination of contrasting flavors and textures. They are best prepared at least 4-6 hours in advance and left at room temperature, to accentuate the flavors of the ingredients.

All recipes are for four portions.

SALSA FROM HELL VERY HOT

This salsa will blow your mind. Serve with grilled steak, tortilla chips, pork, or lamb.

• Make at least 4 hours in advance, and keep at room temperature.

1 onion, minced
1 stalk celery, chopped
5 ripe tomatoes, seeded and chopped
2-3 fresh habañero chilies, minced, or
2-3 dried habañero chilies, soaked
(see page 11) and minced

2 tablespoons chopped fresh cilantro
¹/4-¹/2 teaspoon salt
¹/2 teaspoon cayenne
1 tablespoon lime juice
Freshly ground black pepper

Put all the ingredients into a food processor and briefly blend until fine but not mushy.

MANGO AND CUCUMBER SALSA HOT

This sweet and spicy salsa has a fiery kick. Wonderful with crab, grilled swordfish, or barbecued chicken.

• Make the salsa at least 4-6 hours in advance, and keep at room temperature.

1 large ripe mango, flesh minced
1 heaped tablespoon minced yellow
bell pepper
1 heaped tablespoon minced red bell pepper
Juice of 1 lime

¹/2-1 fresh red scotch bonnet chili, seeded
and minced, or 1 dried habañero chili,
soaked (see page 11) and minced
1 heaped tablespoon chopped fresh cilantro
1 heaped tablespoon peeled and
chopped cucumber

Put all the ingredients into a bowl and mix together well.

Left: Tomato and Mint Salsa

ROASTED PEPPER AND RED ONION SALSA MEDIUM-HOT

This versatile salsa is good with tortilla chips or grilled bruschetta, or tossed with hot pasta.

3 red bell peppers, peeled
(see page 14) and chopped
3 green bell peppers, peeled
(see page 14) and chopped
3 yellow bell peppers, peeled
(see page 14) and chopped

1 small red onion, minced
3 tablespoons extra virgin olive oil
2 tablespoons red wine vinegar
1/2 cup chopped fresh cilantro
2 teaspoons West Indian hot pepper sauce
Salt and freshly ground black pepper

Put all the ingredients into a bowl and mix together well.
Season to taste.

GREEN SALSA VERY HOT

This is a good all-purpose salsa, excellent with grilled swordfish, kebabs, chargrilled shrimp, and tortillas.

• Make the sauce at least 4-6 hours in advance, and keep at room temperture.

7 tomatillos, husks removed, seeded,
and chopped
3 fresh very hot green chilies, minced,
or 1 dried habañero chili, soaked
(see page 11) and minced
1 cup chopped fresh cilantro

6 scallions, minced
Juice of 3 limes
2 cloves garlic, minced
2 tablespoons extra virgin olive oil
1 tablespoon medium sherry
Salt and freshly ground black pepper

Put all the ingredients into a bowl and mix together well.
Season to taste.

TOMATO AND MINT SALSA MEDIUM

This is an irresistible salsa, with a wonderful smoky flavor. Try it with barbecued steak, oysters, tortilla chips, chile con carne, nachos, tacos, beans, and vegetable dishes.

• This salsa is best made 24 hours in advance.

Preheat the oven to 350°F.

6 ripe plum-type tomatoes
2 cloves garlic, minced
1 teaspoon brown sugar
1 1/2 tablespoons tomato paste
1/2 teaspoon balsamic vinegar
2 heaped tablespoons walnut pieces,
lightly toasted (see page 14)
Juice of 1 lime

2 fresh green jalapeño chilies, seeded and
minced, or 2 dried guajillo chilies, soaked,
puréed, and sieved (see page 11)
1/4 cup roughly chopped fresh mint
1 tablespoon chopped fresh rosemary
Grated rind of 1/2 lemon
1/2 teaspoon dried chili flakes
3 tablespoons virgin olive oil
Salt and freshly ground pepper

Place the tomatoes on a baking sheet and roast in the oven until their skins are black. Remove, and put the tomatoes (skins included) in the food processor with the garlic, sugar, tomato paste, and balsamic vinegar. Blend for 1 minute.

Transfer the mixture to a bowl and add the remaining ingredients. Season with salt and pepper. Mix together well, then leave to stand at room temperature (not in the refrigerator) overnight.

RED SALSA MEDIUM-HOT

This is a classic salsa, robust and gutsy, excellent with Mexican dishes such as enchiladas, tortillas, and fresh tortilla chips.

• Let the salsa stand at room temperature for several hours before serving, to enhance the flavors.

1 onion, chopped
1 stalk celery, chopped
5 tomatoes, seeded and chopped
4 fresh red Fresno chilies, minced, or
4 dried ancho chilies, soaked, puréed,
and sieved (see page 11)

2 tablespoons chopped fresh cilantro
1/4-1/2 teaspoon salt
1/4-1/2 teaspoon cayenne
1 tablespoon lime juice
Freshly ground black pepper

Put all the ingredients into a food processor and briefly process to a medium texture; do not overblend.

Season to taste with salt and pepper.

• For a hotter sauce, add a little more minced chili.

Right: Mango and Cucumber Salsa

SALSA PESTO HOT

This salsa will enhance a wide variety of dishes and ingredients. Try it with chargrilled fish or chicken, goat cheese, or tortilla chips, or tossed with hot pasta.

• Make the salsa at least 4-6 hours in advance, and keep at room temperature.

2 fresh hot green chilies, or 1 dried pasado chili, soaked (see page 11)
1 cup pine nuts
1 cup chopped fresh cilantro

3 tablespoons extra virgin olive oil
4 cloves garlic, peeled and minced
Juice of 1 lime
Salt and freshly ground black pepper

Put all the ingredients into the food processor and blend for 30 seconds or until coarse-fine.

MELON SALSA HOT

A delicious combination of hot and cool ingredients, perfect with grilled or roasted meats.

• Make the salsa at least 4-6 hours in advance, and keep at room temperature.

1 cantaloupe melon, skinned, seeded, and chopped
2 fresh hot green chilies, minced, or 5-6 dried tepin chilies, crushed
1 yellow bell pepper, chopped

1 teaspoon extra virgin olive oil
1 teaspoon rice vinegar
Juice of 1 lime
Salt and freshly ground black pepper

Put all the ingredients into the food processor and briefly process to a medium-fine texture; do not overblend.

Season to taste with salt and pepper.

BLACK-BEAN SALSA HOT

This strong salsa can be served as a dish on its own. Or try it with red snapper, grilled lobster, swordfish, and tuna.

• Make the salsa at least 4-6 hours in advance, and keep at room temperature.

1 1/3 cups dried black beans, soaked in water overnight, then drained and cooked until soft but not mushy, or 1 can (16-ounce) black beans, drained
2 tablespoons extra virgin olive oil
1 red bell pepper, chopped
1 yellow bell pepper, chopped
2 cloves garlic, peeled and chopped
Juice of 1 lime

2 heaped tablespoons chopped fresh cilantro
2 thick slices bacon, cooked until crisp, drained, and crumbled
1 fresh hot red chili, minced, or 2 dried chipotle chilies, soaked (see page 11) and minced
2 teaspoons West Indian hot pepper sauce
Sea salt and freshly ground black pepper

Put all the ingredients into a bowl and mix together well. Season to taste with salt and pepper.

BASIC SALSA HOT

Use this classic salsa recipe as the base and add 3/4 pound of your chosen main ingredient. Experiment with tomatoes, tomatillos, papaya, banana, avocados, melon, or cucumber.

• Make the salsa at least 4-6 hours in advance, and keep at room temperature. Can be left overnight.

1 onion, minced
1 stalk celery, chopped
2 tomatoes, seeded and chopped
3 fresh hot green chilies, minced, or 3 dried guajillo chilies, soaked, puréed, and sieved (see page 11) and 1 dried chipotle chili, soaked (see page 11) and minced

2 tablespoons chopped fresh cilantro
1/4-1/2 teaspoon salt
1/4 teaspoon cayenne (more if desired)
1 tablespoon lime juice
Freshly ground black pepper

Put all the ingredients in a food processor and briefly process.

Left: *Melon Salsa*

MARINADES AND PASTES

Marinades and pastes, which are thicker than marinades, are seasoned liquids in which meats, fish, and vegetables are soaked so that they absorb the flavors and, in the case of tougher meats, are tenderized. Most marinades include an acid (the tenderizer) such as lemon juice, vinegar, or wine, as well a selection of herbs and spices. Make marinades in a glass, plastic, ceramic, or stainless steel container; do not use aluminum.

All recipes are for four portions.

SPICED PASTE VERY HOT

Spread this fiery paste over steaks or white-fleshed fish such as skate or sea bass.

2 fresh serrano chilies, or 2 dried ancho chilies, soaked (see page 11) and puréed
2 fresh mild red chilies, or 3 dried New Mexico red chilies, soaked, puréed, and sieved (see page 11)

2 shallots, peeled
4 cloves garlic, peeled
2 tablespoons tomato paste
Juice of 1 lime

Put all the ingredients in a food processor and blend until smooth.

• Marinate ingredients for at least 4 hours, turning occasionally.

ASIAN MARINADE SPICY

The distinctive flavors of ginger, molasses, and honey make this a perfect marinade for barbecued foods. Try it with chicken, fish, seafood, or filet mignon.

1 tablespoon molasses
2 tablespoons honey
1 1/4 cups boiling water
1 1/4 cups shaoxing rice wine or dry sherry

1/2 teaspoon salt
2 teaspoons minced fresh gingerroot
2 tablespoons brown sugar

Put all the ingredients in a bowl and mix together well.

• Marinate ingredients for a least 4-6 hours, turning occasionally.

TANDOORI PASTE SPICY

This aromatic paste is made with more than a dozen ingredients, which accounts for the exotic flavor it gives chicken, lamb chops, or skewered quail.

2 onions, quartered	2 teaspoons ground nutmeg
5 cloves garlic, peeled	2 teaspoons ground cloves
2-inch piece fresh gingerroot, peeled	2 teaspoons ground cinnamon
Juice of 1 lemon	2 teaspoons cayenne
2 teaspoons ground coriander	1/4 cup peanut oil
2 teaspoons ground cumin	1/4 cup sunflower oil
2 teaspoons turmeric	1/4 teaspoon salt
2 teaspoons garam masala	1/4 teaspoon pepper
2 teaspoons ground mace	1 1/4 cups plain yogurt

Put all the ingredients, except the yogurt, in a food processor and blend until a smooth paste is formed. Add the yogurt and blend until well mixed.

• Spread thickly over the ingredients and marinate overnight, turning occasionally.

LEMON AND CHILI MARINADE HOT

This dry marinade really spikes up the flavor of fried fish. Experiment with sardines, strips of sole, or herring roes.

1 teaspoon ground white pepper	2 fresh hot green chilies, chopped, or 2 dried
Grated rind of 1 lemon	habañero chilies, stems removed, crushed
	2 tablespoons cornstarch

Put all the ingredients in a bowl and mix together well.

• For a first course, coat 1 pound small smelt—2 pounds for a main course—in 1 egg white (2 if a main course), then toss in the dry mixture and deep fry. Serve immediately.

• Try the deep-fried fish with a spicy sauce, such as Green Chutney (see page 33) or Spiced Cucumber (see page 34).

SOUTHEAST-ASIAN MARINADE HOT

Hot and spicy, this delicious marinade will enhance the delicate flavors of satay chicken or skewered lamb.

4 cloves garlic, peeled	1 teaspoon curry powder
1 teaspoon freshly ground black pepper	2 small fresh hot red chilies, or 5 dried
2 teaspoons sugar	bird's eye chilies, crushed
2 teaspoons turmeric	1/4 cup peanut or sunflower oil
2 tablespoons chopped fresh cilantro	

Put all the ingredients into a food processor and blend until a smooth paste is formed. Add a little more oil if the mixture is too thick.

• Marinate ingredients overnight, turning occasionally.

MARINADE FOR SPARERIBS

SWEET AND SOUR

Everybody loves this thick, sweet paste on marinated spareribs. Chargrill to enhance the flavor.

3 tablespoons honey	3 tablespoons brown sugar
3 tablespoons light soy sauce	2 tablespoons tomato ketchup
3 tablespoons shaoxing rice wine or dry sherry	6 cloves garlic, peeled and minced

Put all the ingredients into a bowl and mix together well.

• Paint the ribs with marinade and leave in the refrigerator overnight, turning occasionally.

MARINADE FOR SEVICHE MEDIUM

The acid in the lime juice 'cooks' raw fish so that the flesh becomes firmer and turns opaque. Use filets from a really fresh fish such as red snapper, sole, salmon, or tuna or scallops for best results.

2/3 cup fresh lime juice	1 teaspoon freshly ground black pepper
4 scallions, cut into thin, 1-inch strips	2 tablespoons chopped fresh cilantro
1 fresh medium-hot green chili, minced	1/4 cup sunflower oil

Put all the ingredients in a bowl and mix together well.

• Make small cuts into the fish with the tip of a knife to allow the marinade to penetrate the flesh.

• Leave fish to marinate for 3-4 hours or overnight, turning occasionally.

Right: *Marinade for Seviche*

GINGER AND LIME MARINADE SPICY

This versatile marinade is ideal for chicken, beef, or vegetables destined for the barbecue.

1 1/2-inch piece fresh gingerroot,
peeled and minced
5 scallions, white part only, chopped
Grated rind and juice of 2 limes

1 tablespoon five-spice powder
1 tablespoon soy sauce
1 tablespoon sunflower oil

Put all the ingredients in a bowl and mix together well.

• Paint ingredients with the marinade and leave for 4-6 hours or overnight, turning once or twice.

YOGURT MARINADE VERY HOT AND SPICY

This is a hot, full-bodied marinade—just the thing to pep up grilled chicken or lamb.

2 cloves garlic, peeled
1-inch piece fresh gingerroot, peeled
1 tablespoon ground cumin
1/2 teaspoon ground cardamom
1/2 teaspoon chili powder

2 teaspoons paprika
2/3 cup plain yogurt
2 fresh very hot green chilies, seeded and minced, or 2 dried guajillo chilies, soaked, puréed, and sieved (see page 11)

Put the garlic, gingerroot, cumin, cardamom, chili powder, and paprika into the food processor and blend until fine.

Transfer to a bowl, add the yogurt and chilies, and mix together well.

•Place the ingredients into the marinade so they are well covered, and leave overnight.

SINGAPORE MARINADE VERY HOT

Take care—this really is hot. Use to marinate fish, meat, or vegetables to be grilled.

3 tablespoons tomato paste
3 fresh very hot red chilies, or
10 dried bird's eye chilies
6 cloves garlic, peeled
1/2 teaspoon soy sauce

1/2 teaspoon salt
2 tablespoons water
3 tablespoons sunflower oil
Juice of 2 lemons

Put all the ingredients into a food processor and blend until smooth. Transfer the mixture to a saucepan, bring to a boil, and simmer for 2 minutes.

• Marinate ingredients overnight, turning occasionally.

SPICY THAI MARINADE MEDIUM

High in flavor and low in calories, this aromatic marinade is bursting with flavor. Wonderful with chicken or pork ribs.

2 shallots, minced
2 cloves garlic, peeled and minced
2 tablespoons brown sugar
1 tablespoon peanut oil
2 tablespoons fresh lemon juice

3 tablespoons rice vinegar
1 fresh red Thai chili, seeded and minced, or
1-2 dried tepin chilies, crushed
2 tablespoons chopped fresh cilantro
1/2 cup Thai fish sauce

Put all the ingredients into a bowl and let stand at room temperature for at least 1 hour. Then strain and discard the solids.

• Pour the liquid over meat or fish and let marinate overnight.

• Leftover juices can be used for basting.

RELISHES, ATJARS, AND CONFITS

All recipes are for four to six portions.

GRAPE CONFIT SPICY

This confit has a delicate flavor. Serve with foie gras, pâtés, smoked meats, and pork.

2 tablespoons butter
1 onion, sliced
2 teaspoons yellow mustard seeds
1/2 pound seedless grapes

2 tablespoons white wine vinegar or white wine
1 tablespoon sugar

Gently melt the butter in a heavy pan over medium heat and sauté the onion until soft and pale golden.

Add the mustard seeds, grapes, vinegar, and sugar and cook until the liquid has reduced and thickened to a syrupy consistency, about 10 minutes.

SPICED APPLE CHUTNEY MEDIUM AND SPICY

There's something very appealing about spiced apple chutney, especially when it is served with baked ham, cheese, or cold cuts.

2 tablespoons sunflower oil
1 teaspoon cumin seeds
1 onion, sliced
2 apples, cored and roughly chopped

1 fresh medium-hot green chili, minced, or
1 dried pasado chili, soaked (see page 11) and minced
1/3 cup raisins
Salt and freshly ground black pepper

Heat the oil in a heavy pan over medium heat and toast the cumin seeds for 30 seconds, shaking the pan constantly. Add the onion and cook until golden, then add the remaining ingredients and simmer for 15 minutes.

Season with salt and pepper and serve.

CUCUMBER ATJAR spicy

This is a simple recipe. Try it with curry or poached salmon.

1 heaped tablespoon chopped fresh cilantro
1 heaped tablespoon chopped fresh mint
1 shallot, chopped

1/2 English hothouse cucumber, seeded and minced (not peeled)
Juice of 1/2 lime

Put all the ingredients into a bowl and mix together well.

• This atjar makes an excellent cooler for hot curries. Add 1/2–1 cup of plain yogurt, depending on the amount required.

TOASTED COCONUT CHUTNEY MILD

This is a thick, crunchy chutney—the perfect accompaniment for chicken or shellfish curries.

2 tablespoons peanut oil
2 red onions, sliced
1 tablespoon brown sugar
1 tablespoon red wine vinegar
1 fresh mild green chili, seeded and minced, or 1 dried choricero chili, soaked (see page 11) and minced

1/3 cup unsweetened dried shredded coconut, toasted (see page 14)
1/4 teaspoon salt
1/4 teaspoon black pepper

Heat the oil in a heavy pan over medium heat and sauté the onions until very soft and caramel-colored, about 20 minutes.

Turn up the heat, add the sugar and vinegar, and cook until the vinegar has evaporated.

Add the chili and coconut and cook for a further 3-4 minutes, stirring constantly. The mixture should be fairly dry, but stir in a tablespoon of water if it gets too dry. Season to taste.

EGGPLANT RELISH SPICY

This relish has a delicate, subtle flavor. Serve with koftas, chicken and lamb kebabs, and grilled butterflied squab chickens.

1/4 cup olive oil
2 teaspoons cumin seeds
1 eggplant, chopped

2 tomatoes, seeded and chopped
1/3 cup currants
1 1/2 teaspoons salt

Heat the oil in a heavy-based pan over medium heat and toast the cumin seeds for 30 seconds. Quickly add the rest of the ingredients and simmer until the mixture has a thick consistency, about 20 minutes, stirring occasionally.

• If the relish needs to be thicker, cook a few minutes more.

CILANTRO CHUTNEY SPICY

Fresh cilantro gives this chutney a distinctly Asian flavor. Serve with kebabs, samosas, tandooris, and curries.

1/2 pound fresh cilantro
2 tomatoes, cut into 8 wedges each
2 teaspoon cumin seeds
1 teaspoon salt

1 teaspoon garam masala
2 cloves garlic, peeled and minced
2 tablespoons lemon juice
2 tablespoons malt or cider vinegar

Put all the ingredients into a food processor and blend for 30 seconds.

• For mint chutney, substitute fresh mint for the cilantro.

Tomato Relish MEDIUM-HOT

This exceptional tomato relish is delicious with cold lamb, barbecued fish, and grilled tuna.

2 tablespoons olive oil
2 teaspoons yellow mustard seeds
1 onion, sliced
2 cloves garlic, peeled and minced

2 tomatoes, seeded and roughly chopped
Salt and freshly ground black pepper
1 heaped tablespoon fresh basil torn
into strips

Heat the oil in a heavy pan over medium heat and toast the mustard seeds for 30 seconds.

Quickly add the onion and garlic and sauté for 1-2 minutes, taking care not to brown them. Then add the tomatoes and cook for 5 minutes.

Remove from the heat, season with salt and pepper, and stir in the basil.

White-Bean Atjar SPICY

Simple to make, this tasty atjar is excellent with curries, cold cuts, and chicken.

1 tablespoon olive oil
1 teaspoon yellow mustard seeds
1 teaspoon coriander seeds
1 onion, sliced

1 can (16-ounce) cannellini beans, drained
1 tablespoon vinegar
Salt and freshly ground black pepper

Heat the oil in a heavy pan over medium heat and fry the mustard and coriander seeds for 2 minutes, shaking the pan constantly and taking care not to burn them.

Quickly add the onion and sauté until golden, 5-6 minutes.

Add the beans and vinegar and cook until the liquid has almost evaporated.

Remove from the heat and season to taste.

Dried-Fruit Blatjang SWEET AND SOUR

An exotic combination of textures and flavors makes this delicious blatjang a rare treat. Serve with pâtés, cold cuts, sausages, cheese, or pickled fish.

1 pound mixed dried fruits—figs, apricots,
dates, apples, and sour cherries, for example
1/3 cup raisins
1 onion, sliced
1-2 fresh medium-hot red chilies, minced,
or 1-2 dried cascabel chilies, soaked
(see page 11) and the flesh scooped out

2 cloves garlic, peeled and minced
2 cups water
1 1/4 cups malt or cider vinegar
1/2 cup packed brown sugar
1 teaspoon salt

Put all the ingredients in a saucepan and bring to a boil, then turn down the heat and simmer for 30 minutes. Add a little water if the mixture becomes too thick.

Above: Dried-Fruit Blatjang

Hot Yellow-Pepper Relish

HOT AND POWERFUL

Go easy on scotch bonnets as they are very, very hot.

Try this colorful relish with cold roast beef or cold veal, or toss it with hot pasta.

2 yellow bell peppers, quartered
1/2-1 fresh scotch bonnet chili, seeded
2 tablespoons olive oil

1 heaped tablespoon chopped fresh cilantro
Salt and freshly ground black pepper

Put the yellow bell peppers under a hot broiler, skin side up, and cook until the skins turn black. Remove from the broiler, let cool, and then peel. (Alternatively, leave the skins on; they have a lovely "charred" taste.)

Put the chili under the broiler and cook until the skin turns black. Remove from the broiler, but leave the skin on.

Put all the ingredients into a food processor and briefly blend until very fine.

ACKNOWLEDGMENTS

I have had the good fortune to work with a team whose energy, enthusiasm and sense of humor have proved second to none. I would like to thank all of them for playing their parts with such expertise and exuberance.

In particular, I am indebted to Rose Prince, whose culinary skills have been invaluable. She gave her time so generously and was such a pleasure to work with that I inevitably look forward to other projects. Thanks also to Jose Luke, who, along with Rose, tried and tested virtually all the recipes and made them look so tempting for the photographs.

To my assistant Christopher Leach, who has rushed around, almost demonically, for weeks, fetching and carrying anything from tables to teacups. His contribution has been zestful yet always practical. I would also like to thank my friend Simon Wheeler for his outstandingly beautiful photographs—they make the book.

Last but not least my sincere thanks to the following companies for loaning and supplying food and props for photography: Cool Chile Co.; Tawana Oriental Supermarket; Peking Supermarket; Designers Guild; Joss Graham Oriental Textiles; William Sheppee Ltd; Ceramica Blue; William Yeoward; Summerill & Bishop; Mosaik; Robert Budwig; Madelaine Adams; Fired Earth; Verandah; Sylvia Napier Antiques.

RECIPE INDEX

First published in The United States of America in 1995
by Rizzoli International Publications, Inc.
300 Park Avenue South, New York, NY 10010

First published in Great Britain in 1995 by
George Weidenfeld & Nicolson Limited
The Orion Publishing Group

ISBN 0-8478-1874-8

LC 95-67211

Designed by Thumb Design Partnership

Printed and bound in Italy